Perfect is not Pretty

TABLE OF CONTENTS

ACKNOWLEDGEMENTS

TRUE MEANING OF PERFECT
MATURITY
"OH DEATH, WHERE ART THOU STING"
SPORT ANALOGY
SWEAT THEN GLORY
THE 110
THE 120
SUFFERING FOR A SEASON
BIBLICAL SIGNIFICANCE
THE BREAKDOWN
PYSICAL FREEDOM VS. MENTAL FREEDOM
THE BUILDUP
THE FRUITFUL REWARD
BIBLICAL PERFECTION
BRAINS—PAUL
THE TYRANT
THE TRANSFORMATION
THE TEACHER
BRONZE—SAMPSON
THE BABY
THE BULLY
THE BEREAVED
BEAUTY—MARY
THE BEAUTY WITHIN
THE PERFECT ROAD TO THE CROSS
JESUS THE CHRIST

LIST OF THANKS

DEDICATION

    This book is predominately dedicated to my late daughters Kellie Sarai Williams & Chelsea Cenora Williams. They graced me with a beauty that comes from deep within. They gave me something that I could give to the world which was the strength that loosed me from the sting of death. I can now boldly give the world the Words of Christ without fear. I love you babies, and you done your duty while on your brief stay here on Earth. Thank you for the moments we did share.

'The True Meaning of Perfect'

Knowing this that the trying of your faith worketh patience. But let patience have her perfect work, that ye may perfect and entire, wanting nothing. (James 1:3-4)

There have been many translations since the days that the apostles wrote their books of the Bible. There have been many nations to come into rule since the days that Jesus walked the Earth. This being known, we must understand that some words may have lost its strength from what was the original meaning. Some words may have been lost as well as changed entirely within our western hemisphere dialect. I only want to deal with the word 'perfect' that was used within the context from the book of James.

The Merriam-Webster dictionary has several meanings of the word perfect. The first meaning says being without fault or defect[1]. This is obviously not what James could have meant unless he wanted to be contrary with the scripture that says there is none righteous, no not one. Webster dictionary also says perfect means exact, precise[2]. Well I want to use the third meaning that says complete[3]. This translation is closest to the Greek word of 'teleios' which means completeness (in various applications of labor, growth, mental and moral character, etc.)[4] I really think the New American Bible's translation hits home by saying the word mature[5]. The New Living Translation mentions the word perfect as being strong in character[6]. These latter translations should help our understanding that it's not the Western's understanding of perfect but through our trials and tribulations endurance will bring about maturity. When we mature from situations, we should react differently to those situations when they come about again. For example, if we still get upset over a situation that we went through five years earlier, well we must not have matured. There should be some evidence of change after enduring something.

Maturity

According to the Merriam-Webster Dictionary, the root word for maturity, (mature), means: having attained a final or desired state, of or relating to a condition of full development, and to reach or bring to maturity or completion.[7] The word maturity itself, as stated by the same dictionary, defines maturity as full development.[8] These are quite accurate when lining up with my message of maturing as a Christian. Without this maturity, we will have a hard time witnessing to the World about a heavenly kingdom on Earth. That message means that our mindset should have our bodies and actions reacting differently than the world's mindset of actions.

What I'm trying to get across is the fact that if we want to obtain a sense of true holiness that resembles Christ Jesus; we must behave as a follower of Him as well. This state of being that He portrayed comes with a price. This was mentioned in my title, perfect, (mature), is not pretty. Pretty declares that we must go through trials and tribulations to have the manifestations of being mature.

Have you ever wondered why the elderly seems not to stress out or fuss about many things? I wondered until I started maturing myself and understanding that it is a state of mindset which prevents me from stressing out on so many trivial subjects in life. There should be a point in a person's life that the older one gets, the less fighting and arguing should occur within one's lives. The book of Proverbs has so many wise sayings about how to handle a foolish person. The teachings are there to prevent falling into strife with people who have not matured. If we descend into someone's bickering and complaining and begin to do the same, well that lets us know that we are not mature ourselves. I

Perfect is not Pretty

have had many years during which fellow co-workers have wondered where I got my patience and maturity from, considering that I was quite younger the majority of times. That was always my time to explain to them about Christ and His teachings. Displaying maturity has become a more useful tool than any other witness strategy that I have encountered. People do really want to live a more peaceful life. This is one of my missions, throughout this book and many to follow is to show people how to obtain peace within a sinful world's mindset. Becoming mature can stretch our minds and thoughts farther than we can imagine it to be stretched. It will cause us to be challenged way beyond what we are accustomed to. It may mean for most of us to *'bite our tongues'* or just hold our peace when we know we are right. The Holy Bible teaches that for peace sakes to allow others to have the little victory because God our Father sees all and will reward us for giving in to the small things. The return is a greater reward for us by furthering the kingdom of God through our humility in the world. Our light has to shine in this dark generation we currently live in. We are the hope for many souls that need to become saved through our actions.

Therefore, from reading thus far, if you want to change and have a more peaceful end, you should continue reading to help yourself obtain that peaceful mindset. If, however, you are still stubborn and don't want to change or go through the process of being humbled: well I guess you need to put this book down for now and find some fiction that will help you cope with the cruel state of this sinful generation. As for me and my house, we shall follow the Lord.[9]

Oh Death, Where Art Thou Sting?

Spring 2004 brought a beautiful baby girl into the world, though only for a short season. Many times we do not know why things happen to us or for us. Having a relationship with God can cut down on many of the not knowing, but there will always be some unknown when dealing with God. Some situations may be understood immediately, some a short season, and some a long season away. Unfortunately, it is the ones we never understand during our lives that we have the most trouble dealing with. I try to always look for reasons that God does things, yet I'm not always successful. This is where our faith must come in and comfort us or we can stray away from God due to disappointments.

The book of Job gives us strength on handling the unknown 'whys' that we have to deal with in life. Like Job, we must just take the bad along with the good and trust in the almighty God. By me being a 'thinker,' I like for God to give me reasons for everything he does to me. I do have enough sense that my Father does not have to explain everything to me. Sometimes I just have to just trust and lean to His understanding and not my own.

Many people are in bondage to fear. Many fears are in this world, but I want to speak about the fear of death. The Enemy wants to keep us in bondage to death to try and keep us away from the love of God. I can honestly say that God's ways are definitely not our ways. I also can testify to the scripture that mentions that all things work for the good of those that love Him. I have been through so much tragedy that I and many others wonder why I have not committed suicide by this time. Don't think I have not entertained the idea, but God had me even when I didn't know Him. I have hated many trials, but the love from God has helped me endure. I have hit rock bottom to the point I couldn't love anyone or anything anymore. It seemed that even when God blessed me finally to love again by giving me my son Josiah that tragedy still lurked around the corner. When he was born, I had to name him Josiah, meaning Jehovah heals, because my heart was finally healed from the hurt of love. I truly loved again when he was born. I thanked God so much that I even named his middle name Emmanuel, meaning God with us. After two years of marital struggles, came the third year of career troubles and finally the spring that brought joy and eventually unbelievable weight that I thought could never be lifted. When my daughter Sarai was given to me for a moment and returned to the father, I couldn't be hurt anymore it seemed. Since that moment in time, I've feared no more. Sure, I had disappointments afterwards, but I could never be hurt tremendously anymore because I didn't even fear death anymore.

God forbid that anyone must go through so much tragedy to get to the point of no fear, but as for me, that seemed to be the final weight to break my back. Bouncing back from that could only take the love of God. I felt like I could never have any more joy because of all the tragedy that haunted my life. I felt like I could never lift the name of the LORD to anyone ever again. It was at that time that I understood the scripture mentioning that in our weakness He is made strong. It didn't last but three days until I had to minister to another individual about Christ. I couldn't think of my sorrows since that I was trying to help someone else out of their tragedy. Only this time, and from that moment on, I had a new boldness of witnessing about the power of the one and only true living God. This was an understanding that could not be explained. God gave me a peace that surpassed all understanding; and because of that, I in return have preached His Word with no fear of anyone or anything. I know that there is something out there that is unexplainable and is empowering me to go on in this cruel world that is losing love and preach the Good News that Jesus is Lord and has risen from the dead to sit on the right hand of the LORD of Host.

Mr. Charles Williams Jr

I don't know what my destiny will hold, but as for now, I feel as Paul explained in the book of Philippians that for me to live is Christ and to die is gain. I would much rather be away from the pain in this world and be with the Lord; yet while I am in the land of the living, I will preach His Word to help others. The fear of death cannot rule over me because I know that death will only bring me closer to the Lord in the sense that I know that my salvation is secure in Him. That being understood, how can I fear what an enemy can do to me? That being noted, how can I fear someone who can only destroy my physical body when there is someone who can kill my body and soul? Jesus is the reason I live. Man has, will, and currently still is disappointing me, but that is the reason my trust is in the LORD and not unto mankind.

I am mentioning this chapter because there should come a time that Jesus becomes your Lord and not just your Savior. Jesus should be your source of life. When we make that choice in our lives, God will use the gift that he put into you and using that gift will be your satisfaction and drive to live. At that point, not even death will have any power over you to drive a wedge between you and God. When our lives are hidden in Christ, sin has no rule over us to usher us into death, or rather an eternal separation from God. Giving our lives to Christ will help you to conquer the fear that death will separate you from God. My boldness in Christ comes from asking death, "where is your sting"?

'Sweat then Glory'

For our light affliction, which is but for a moment, work for us a far more exceeding and eternal weight of glory.   (2 Corinthians 3:1)

Ready, set, go; and 37 seconds later comes the glory of seeing the fruit of my labor from months of training. Oh my, the love of everyone to see me cross the finish line ahead of the pack. It can be a truly wonderful feeling. Along with the cheers comes expectation to win. I really can't blame their reactions, but I wonder did they know what I had to endure to arrive at that point. I almost come to the position sometimes to say that old, wise saying, 'don't put the cart before the horse.' Why do I say that? I say that because the '*sweat comes before the glory*.'

That walk of life of my track and field days prepared me to walk accordingly in the ministry of Christ. Although it was my gift to be able to retain the words of God, I had to exercise that gift to arrive at this point of maturity. After being ministered to from my Grandmother while a sinner, I ran toward God and started reading His Word one December night of 1994. I didn't pause from reading his Word until six months later after reading from Genesis to Revelation. I had to continue to labor with bible studies, fellowshipping and prayer all while still learning the Word. So now when people desire this fruit that is evident due to the working of the body of Christ, I can appreciate the sweat that has led to this glory. Yet the people will not understand the spiritual arrival unless I also tell my carnal story.

Many people on my own track team could not understand why I would stay after practice and continue to train. Fellow track runners didn't think it took *'all that'* when I would run on the weekends as well. It seems that something would always be said during the training sessions that I endured. If truth is told, even I said discouraging words from time to time while training. It wasn't until the junior year that I would finally lay all that negative motivation to the side. I would just get my good sweat on and move on. I by then had understood that it took that sweat to receive the rewards I had obtained during my freshman and sophomore years. Amazingly I noticed that after I had stopped the complaining and receiving that negativity from my own teammates that I began receiving a multitude of rewards and even my own teammates started to run on the weekends with me. I also had three dedicated guys that did all the extra work required and believed in me that it was necessary to labor so hard to be worthy of the prize that we were pursuing.

We did receive that glory in the form of being the fastest mile relay team to run in the meet of champions that year. This was one of the glories that we planned from day one of that spring training that year. Yes, it was hard, and yes it felt every bit of being worth it. I had received numerous other prizes that year, but this was by far the greatest because I could share it with others.

This is a parallel walk to the walk that we have in Christ Jesus to endure. The glory that is seen in others, such as famous preachers, and singers, evangelist, etc...., takes a walk of sweating that most never see or could even comprehend. A walk that if others knew, they would never want to reach that plateau of the ones they desire to be like.

There is an adage that says, 'anything worth having is worth fighting for.' The glorious gift of God is something worthy to possess and worth laboring for.

'The 110'

    I always knew while growing up that I had more energy than the next person. I would run farther, play longer, and endure to the end no matter what the sport may be. My best friend Billy and I would play everything from basketball to squash, from chopping wood to riding bikes, from anything to everything that required a no quit attitude. I always knew I had to train harder to be successful and had a made-up mind to be determined never to quit.

    My first season running the 110 intermediate hurdles as a freshman in high school, (although during those times freshmen were still considered Jr. High school), was quite challenging. As all typical hurdlers at that age in a small town, hurdling was not a trained skill that many coaches had knowledge about. I was fortunate enough to manage a victory but oh what an awful timed result. I was privileged in that the High School coach noticed greatness in me when I couldn't even imagine what I was able to accomplish. He was only there in Blytheville for two seasons, just long enough to impart into me something compelling. He showed me the will to work toward a goal. The coach took me under his wing and trained me during the last class period of athletics. I would leave the junior high school and train at the high school over hurdles during class time. I would train with the high school boys after hurdle practice which didn't matter much since I could outrun the high school boys as well. As I proceeded to learn more about the hurdles, my times began to lower. I came to the realization that training mixed with time was beneficial to obtain good results. This understanding spurred me on to train longer and wiser in all areas of track and field. Once again, as a result, I improved my times in all other areas as well.

Mr. Charles Williams Jr

There are times in life when we will make decisions that will change, or I could even say alter, the rest of one's life. I made a choice to be more serious about something (track and field) than the next person. That one decision set my life on track of becoming a notarized sports figure. Coupled with my determination to finish what I started, I proceeded to embrace the moments of sweating. I am mentioning these qualities because the same way they helped me in my spiritual life, I want to convey them to others to aid in their spiritual lives as well. Qualities learned such as determination, character, perseverance, and many others like these have helped me in more ways than track and field, but the field of life just as well. Without these qualities, I would not have understood that the sweat was working toward a greater prize further down the road. Without these qualities, I would have quite often due to the lack thereof.

I remember the days of not wanting to jog over to the high school during the 7th class period. I had to learn that it would be many days of jogging alone if I wanted to get what I wanted out of life, at least dealing with track. So, I jogged alone for months and eventually years afterward. I came to realize that on the level I wanted to perform, I had to go through, even if it meant going through alone. This is the resemblance I carried over into my spiritual life. I endured many bible studying on my own, and small beginnings in Sunday school as well as weekday bible training. Thank goodness I had something to look back on when days like that became real.

The ironic thing about all of this is that I didn't know until many years later how that all those characteristics mentioned earlier were helping others through many of their own situations. That drive, and determination were told to me that it 'fired up,' or rather, pulled many others through to run longer in track and hold on longer during life's trials. So, I guess it's true that you never know who's watching or that someone is always watching. This is a good reason why we should never give up so quickly and use any situation in life that can be turned around to produce something positive.

'The 120'

Seeing how my 110 hurdles career was broken down by various training seasons helped me understand the maturing of Moses during his lifelong journey. I call this section the '120' by breaking down his journey of three different forty years' events. The first forty years were spent in Egypt in Pharaoh's house. Under the tutelage of the Egyptians, Moses became a 'learned' man and became skilled in many areas that would be needful throughout his life. Many times we did not understand when growing up that our parents might just know what they are doing when they thrust upon us things that make no sense to us at an early age. Doing things as simple as keeping your room clean builds character in cleanliness that's needed when mom is no longer around to clean for you. Keeping your room clean also fights off the awful spirit of slothfulness/laziness. Chores like taking out the trash and washing dishes fall under the same category of character building. Parents are so resourceful that they may even train you in a fun way, such as playing doctor, house, and other role-playing games to help guide you into professions for a career to sustain your life. Sending you to Boys/Girls Scout, summer camps, and other extra-curricular activities to broaden your horizons outside of the mere two block radius of your neighborhood.

All these things your parents do because of what they see in you and wanting the best for you. If mortal parents would do this for you out of love, what about your Father in Heaven and His Agape love which is the highest form of love? God had heard the cries of His children, the Israelites, and provided a chosen vessel in Moses to deliver God's people out of bondage. We can't forget how wiser God is compared to our parents so we know that God would not send someone unprepared to carry out His plan. Moses was scheduled to learn the ways of the Egyptian's knowledge in math and science, and warfare and survival. All these things were going to work for the good of God's people who loved and longed for God's attention. So Moses first forty years was helpful for the guidance of hundreds of thousands of people to be delivered. That was definitely considered crowd control.

  The next forty years were predominately for Moses to learn how to lead many sheep and learn how to be humble. Moses had to understand that his life was sparred as a child for the sake of God's people. Moses had to realize that pride had no place in God's plans. Moses also had to learn that delivering God's people had to be done God's way and not man's way. If we really think about it, Christians try to solve many problems using human wisdom. It doesn't seem to hold fast. Even Moses tried to free God's people his way but learned soon afterward that his way could not release his people. When we use God's wisdom to solve problems they hold fast. Moses learned that by dwelling on the backside of the wilderness for forty years. Moses was humbled, and then God prepared their meeting that would change his life's plans and residence once more. As we grow in the Lord, our will changes to His will. The remarkable thing is that He never forces us to change. Out of either love for Him, or frustration from the world, we seem to surrender all to Him one way or another.

The joyful twist is that it feels so much better to let Him handle the burdens; afterward, we want to kick ourselves in the rear for not letting Him take over our lives sooner. Having God in the driver's seat allows for a more prosperous journey. Moses final forty years was still an even more learning process. The difference of his later years was the fact that he journeyed knowing that God was with Him and in control of his life. Moses became the epitome of leadership. After eighty years of training his leadership skills became evident. We seem to mirror the predominately same journey as Moses in growth with the LORD. As I look back over my life, I too can see how more prosperous walking with the LORD was compared to walking without Him.

Mr. Charles Williams Jr

We may not live as long as Moses and hopefully not take so long on each shift to another level with God, but I want everyone to understand the walk with God as the importance of it all. Many people reverenced Moses in times past and even still today due to the accomplishments of his latter forty years; but oh how I hope I can impart the importance that the perfection or should I say the maturity of Moses' walk with God did not come from an overnight journey. The labor that he endured was not pretty; therefore I say 'perfect is not pretty.'

Suffering for a Season

Now no chastening for the present seemeth to be joyous, but grievous; nevertheless afterward it yieldeth the peaceable fruit of righteousness unto them which are exercised thereby (Hebrews 12:11)

At the age of seventeen, I joined the Army Reserves while still in high school. The Army had created a program called 'split training.' This entailed an individual going to basic training during the summer vacation from high school and returning to training the following year after graduation. This became a turning point in my life. I gained so much from my Army experience that it spilled over into my personal life. I grew in strength, character, and wisdom.

For starters, I naturally grew in strength due to the morning physical training hours. By me being a track athlete, I craved the workouts because I knew it would benefit me for my next season. The push-ups and sit-ups gave me strength as well as pack on more muscle onto my small frame. I went into the military weighing around 142lbs. Between the workouts and the healthy 3 square meals a day, I returned home weighing 156lbs and with some serious muscle definitions. Don't let it sound like it was all cookies and milk while working out because it was challenging. I learned what muscle failure was and I didn't particularly like it. A person does not see the end results while going through. Many mornings I dreaded getting up to go physical training (PT). Many mornings I returned from PT extremely exhausted. I really didn't notice the results until I returned home and received the compliments from others of my physical stature.

I also was enrolled in the R.O.T.C. program at the high school for all three years. I was a part of the drill team for all three years as well. I became the commander of the rifle drill team before leaving for basic training, and it was beneficial for me when I returned. No one on the rifle drill team could do more push-ups than I could. Push-ups became a form of discipline to sharpen the skills of drills. Little did they know that through the competition of trying to do more push-ups than I could, this would become beneficial for them. We became hugely successful that year, and through the discipline that I bestowed upon them, we were invited to perform all over the area. The team didn't know how suffering with the late night hours and the weekend training would come to play a significant factor in their having success. I was proud of the team, and the school was proud of us as well.

My character became noticeable immediately at home first. I was no longer the little brother that tended to be lazy in many areas. I was up at the break of dawn leaving the house to go jogging before school. My bedroom and bed were always tidy since my return. My hygiene became first-rate, and there were no more fussing from my older sister about cleaning up the bathroom when finished.

At school, I became a role model for the senior class in many ways. I showed respect for all teachers within the classroom. I commanded my drill team to practice out front for all students to see the discipline one could have if willing to work for it. Within the R.O.T.C. classroom my character, along with good grades, landed me commander for the classroom as well. Even my grade point average increased due to paying more attention to my schoolwork and buckling down on my studies overall. I became disciplined in the area of healthy eating as well. I was in control of my healthy habits and would rarely do anything in the field of partying too much, and all that comes along with it. I really appreciated that change in my life. I'm sure others recognized it as well.

    I grew up as well while gone for the summer. I guess you could say that I became a man while gone. When I returned I supported myself outside of house bills. I bought all of my clothing and extra snacks. I paid my way to any extracurricular activities throughout the year. I had obtained wisdom while in basic training about the importance of performing well in life. I made a lot of good choices in my senior year compared to the prior years of my life. A lot of silliness fled from my presence and was replaced with wise decisions. Scripture says that *when I was a child, I spake as a child, I understood as a child, I thought as a child: but when I became a man, I put away childish things*[10]. I knew that I wanted to go to college and my actions would reflect upon me getting into college. I was determined to make it regardless of what nonsense my peers wanted to do. I had learned to say no in the face of foolishness. I had become a man and made my choices based on what 'I' wanted and needed to do and not on following what others wanted to do.

So overall I understood that suffering brings about a much-needed change and that I shouldn't dislike suffering but that I should welcome it into my life. At the beginning of the book of James, James mentions that we should count it all joy when we fall into various situations because it brings about maturity. So I thank the suffering for a season to obtain the outcome I received in track and field. I went from average times, heights, and distances to outdoing the whole state in many areas. I held the number one spot throughout the year in several areas. I was within the top three in all events I participated in, except for the long jump where I hovered around in the eight positions. I participated in five events each track meet and six events when in Missouri and Tennessee and I never had less than three 1st place finishes each competition. This was all while averaging at least four 1st places every contest. Thank goodness for the suffering for a season.

The Breakdown

The Israelites went through a period that I call 'boot camp.' There 'boot camp' followed what the purpose of the military's camp was as well. The military's goal was to breakdown one's traditional way of thinking to eventually rise up a new way of thinking to bring about a more effective way of functioning. It really makes sense if you think about it. The military needs a standard way of thinking since there are so many different individuals that make up the armed forces. The only way for hundreds of thousands of men to move in the same direction is to have a familiar standard for all to follow. As a matter of fact, even nature does the same as well just by looking at an army of ants. So to receive a fruitful reward, many must have the same mindset to perform the desired task. It has been proven effective that the old way has to be broken down and then rebuilt to a new way of thinking and afterward a reward can be achieved.

At first glance at the children of Israel, I thought they were just outright rebellious and clueless people. After reading the great miracle of the parting of the Red Sea, I just couldn't understand their actions of later rebellion and doubt. I kept saying "how can someone witness a miracle like that and still have problems believing and trusting in the LORD"? They were fed straight from heaven for forty years with Manna. Their clothing and shoes did not wear out. I began to reflect on my basic military training and started to realize what God was doing. Once I took my focus off of the children of Israel, I started noticing God's strategy. He was breaking down the children of Israel's ideas such as the foreign idols saving them. God was making them rely entirely on Him and none other. He had to break down that dependency on the multitude of false gods and vain sacrifices. Many fell dead in

Perfect is not Pretty

the desert when rebellion occurred. It was God's way or perish. Once the children of Israel understood that concept, they began to accept God's way of thinking, which lead to life, and no longer relied on their false beliefs but for the faith in the One and Only True Living God of their forefather Israel.

I'm not going to sugar coat the idea that breakdown is easy, yet I will be an advocate for standing and saying that it is effective. As I mentioned earlier, many fell dead due to rebellion and doubt. When they reached the 'gateway' to the promise land during Moses lifetime, the ones that were twenty years of age and older were the responsible ones that got the Israelites to lose out on their blessings and returned to wander in the desert's 'boot camp.' These would not see the promise land again, but the ones younger would possess the land. I wanted to mention this in this manner because of the advice I wanted to give to the youth: *Seek ye the LORD while he may be found, call ye upon him while He is near*[11]. Also, I have to ask, *For what is a man profited, if he shall gain the whole world, and lose his own soul; or what shall a man give in exchange for his soul*[12]? Younger children can have so much of God early on if they would just follow Him the day that they hear His voice and harden not their hearts.

    I don't know if many people realize that the children of Israel lived in bondage in a foreign land for four hundred and thirty years. After such a long time, one can pick up habits that were at one time not accepted among God's people. Israel began knowing idols, sacrifices, and altogether a strange way of living that was contrary to Israel's God. Although they eventually left Egypt physically, they had problems leaving the mentality of slavery, sacrifices, and the strange way of living behind. Although they obtained their freedom physically, they ultimately enslaved themselves in their minds till death. I used to be baffled by the rebellion and doubt that the Israelites had until I had to realize that freedom from the mind is more difficult than physical freedom.

Mr. Charles Williams Jr

Physical Freedom vs. Mental Freedom

    The old saying 'a mind is a terrible thing to waste' can be overlooked if not careful. Although many of the Israelites perished in the wilderness, their children were saved by them at least leaving Egypt (bondage). Many people today may be still in bondage although physically free. Situations like an abused woman may have been finally freed from the abusive relationship she was in by moving to a shelter for battered women yet at the same time she continues to have fear rule over her life. It may be a knock on the door, a car screech, or even a simple hello from behind that manifest the fear from within. I am by no way taking the effect of abuse lightly; but by no means will I stay silent on what is really taking place. That being noted let's first be in agreement on that way of thinking must be broken down so a build-up can then take place. I will address this matter in the next chapter.

    I first want to mention another physical vs. mental freedom that needs to be discussed. I have seen so many people get out of the physical bondage of poverty by various means but was never delivered from the mental bondage of poverty. If you say how is that so; well let's look at the fact that through various ways we know some people have escaped poverty through means of lotteries. Some have avoided the mechanisms of poverty through stardom (acting, music, etc..,). We have seen those same individuals return to poverty shortly after that because they didn't free their mind and train their minds on how to handle the wealth. The *poverty mentality* spent the wealth on depreciated items such as cars, fast living, clothes and shoes, and wasteful items thereof. A *freed* mind would dwell on appreciated values items such as homes, insurance, stocks and bonds, savings accounts and such thereof. Even a spiritual and moral value of things would be helpful such as giving to churches and charitable organizations would return unto them by whatever way one may label it; such as karma, 'what goes around comes around', the law of seedtime and harvest, and of course the all-time favorite 'reaping and sowing'.

'The Build Up'

For the first five weeks of basic training, I thought the Drill Sergeants to be the enemy. From the moment of stepping off the 'cattle car' that transported us to our new home for the summer, the intimidation had begun and didn't let up for weeks. It wasn't until it was time to practice on the shooting range with the rifles did I see the other side of the Drill Sergeants.

I have first to mention that I, along with four others, was an exception to walking out to the ranges. I was assigned to ammo detail which meant that I was not confined to the running portion of morning physical therapy (PT). When others went to do the running part of PT, the ammo detail went to eat, shower, and get dressed to ride out to the range. I got a break by not having to walk out to the range every day. For the first time, I started seeing the Drill Sergeants as real human beings and not the hardcore mean monsters that yell at us every day. I began to learn the purpose of the yelling and breakdown of our ways of thoughts. The Drill Sergeants at the range began teaching the privates on ammo detail about the military and the ammo, and most of all about life. I began to see why they thought the way they did and why we couldn't continue to think individually as we did.

    As the weeks continued on, the Drill Sergeants began to loosen up on the yelling and began to teach and sometimes even gave us reasons why they yelled or instructed us to do things. It became more natural for them to explain things to us because we began to think alike and have the same purpose in mind. There were fewer individual mindsets around as in the beginning, and now we started to think and move as a group. This training showed me that to move effectively we had to think on the same 'page.' I never would've thought that the Drill Sergeants had my best interest in mind from their actions of the first few weeks of basic training. Now I understand that they had to get rid of that individualized, prideful thinking that most of us had inside of us. Although I had some of that corrupt thinking, I had fortunately been involved in many team sports, so there wasn't too much fuss from me about teamwork. I did have a huge problem with authority yelling at me because I had never really experienced it, but I had to deal with it.

All throughout sports, I tended to be exceptional and the Coaches never really got onto my case. If they did get onto me, they managed not to yell at me. A couple of times I remember that when I was yelled at I chose to quit the team. I never had a father in the home to teach me to deal with negative emotions; let alone about someone chastising me. This was, I would definitely say, the biggest problem I had growing up. I didn't understand that chastening was actually a good thing. All this being said I want to convey that the chastening is an ok and needed process of life. The Bible says in the book of Hebrews chapter 12 verse 11 that '...no chastening for the present seems to be joyous, but grievous: nevertheless afterward it yields the peaceable fruit of righteousness unto them which are exercised thereby". We have to look down the road if we want to have good results in whatever we do. Chastening can be the buildup if we change our perspective. I always talk to my son about correction. I still explain to him that if there is a behavior that I do not want him to perform I must use corrective measures to stop that behavior and build on a more decisive action. I didn't have that luxury of explanation when I was growing up. I was punished with no comment about the significance of a corrective behavior.

    God had decided that through the 'wilderness boot camp' that the children of Israel had to be broken down about the false beliefs in idols. They then needed to rebuild their faith in Him. Before the experience of Mt. Sinai with the Ten Commandments, the Israelites did not have set rules about how to live for God. On Mt. Sinai the Israelites were exposed directly to just how the LORD wanted them to behave. His set rules would be the building up of a nation of people that would eventually set the tone of following the one true God throughout the rest of Earth's days. Here we are today after thousands of years with a society that has written laws that reflect the Ten Commandments. This very nation of the Americas was built upon these very same laws.

At a young age, many people can't see that rules are for the good and not made up to be cruel. Some young ones even believe that parents and people in positions of authority actually make up rules to take away fun activities to make the young ones have a miserable life under their jurisdiction. This causes teenagers to rush to grow up and get out on their own so they can live their own life and do whatever they want to do. Unfortunately, after a few months of real life, of their so-called 'independence,' they find out there are still rules to be followed in life. Many people try the same thing by avoiding the teachings of the Holy Bible just to find out after many years of suffering that the Bible was the best thing for their lives. This is why I wanted so much to write books so that many more, other than within my own congregation, would be blessed early in life about the Word of God. I don't want any troubles to come upon people if it can be avoided. I don't have to use cocaine to understand that cocaine can trouble my life greatly. This is how I want to help others by exposing God's love to them before they try the world's ways of living that can lead to so many sorrows and tormenting. The Bible mentions in Romans 15:4 that the scriptures were written aforetime for our learning. Therefore I urge you to dive into the Word of God and learn lessons from reading. I always tell others while teaching that I don't have to be a drug addict to know that I don't want to become a drug addict. I can just watch others that are addicted to knowing I don't want to become addicted. I wish you also to learn lessons from reading.

After forty years of wandering in the wilderness, the Israelites were finally ready to walk into the promised land of long ago. They had walked with God for forty years and seen many of His miracles that showed His provisions and power. They were ready to conquer other nations and show the world that there was a one and true living God; not one fastened by nails and overlaid with gold and silver. The giants that struck fear in their hearts forty years earlier were no longer a factor due to the building up that the LORD placed within their hearts. Now the secure walls of Jericho would tumble down not by hands but by faith. By faith, the LORD would fight their battles for them and give the Israelites the recognition so that all the nations would fear their God.

The Fruitful Reward

One year to go to graduation. What will my senior year be like? Well, it was all up to me. I've had a life-altering summer before my senior year. What will I do with it? What will be my fruits? That high school coach had given me more than skills of jumping hurdles. He had given me a spark of discipline that pushed myself to not quit on myself because of a little chastening. I had to look back on those ninth grade training sessions with him to help me take on the harshness of the Drill Sergeants. Well, it helped much. I was able to endure the pressures from the Drill Sergeants as well as the five o'clock morning workouts. I also braved the temperatures of more than one hundred degrees weather of South Carolina in July. I could almost say that training back in Arkansas during late winter and spring was a piece of cake. I went from placing around fourth place in events such as high jumping, long jumping, mile relays and sometimes 110 hurdles to placing first in all except for maybe 2nd and 3rd in the long jump. I went from jumping 6' 2" in the high jump to 6' 9" in one season. I broke records in every meet and one meet I broke four while in another I broke five in one day. While most young men would love to participate in at least one event at the Meet of Champions, I had the honor of attending in four. Winning in the meet of Champions placed me in an elite field throughout the nation as a 'Blue Chipper.' My time was the ninth fastest in the whole nation. I signed my letter of intent at the end of spring to run for the Nation's number one track and field program, the Arkansas Razorbacks. While running there my first outdoor season, I was apart of a World Record relay team. That record stood for over fifteen years. We never know what an outcome could be if we never are willing to go through something to get there. I did my suffering for a season to get the desired result that was worthy of my labor. I wish to push others to go the extra mile and endure what may lie ahead to achieve a much greater reward at the other end of perseverance.

After the wilderness experience, came the Joshua Generation. A generation that conquered many nations with the fear of the LORD reigning over the whole world was the result of what the Israelites went through in the wilderness. There are millions of people that have become followers of the God of Israel because of their plight. Billions have been affected throughout this world because of them. We have to ask ourselves "who can we affect by going through and coming out to become prosperous as a better human being." We have to come to some point in life and realize that we have to go through to become 'perfect,' or a better translation is mature. Through maturity, we should tend not to act as though we are that younger person that had no self-control. Without that self-control, we will literally tear our lives down. The Bible tells of a woman without self-control is a foolish woman and will tear down her home. The Bible tells us a person without self-control is like a city without walls. Aren't you tired of destruction becoming evident in your life? We have to be honest and know that we have to work toward perfection. We have to stop looking at people and thinking that the perfect that you see came overnight. Every successful person should have a story to tell about how they became the 'perfect' person in our sight. Maturity comes from going through something. So let's be honest with ourselves and understand that there is a process which must take place before the fruitful reward of success.

Biblical Perfection

¹¹If, therefore, perfection were by the Levitical priesthood, (for under it the people received the law,) what further need was there that another priest should rise after the order of Melchisedec, and not be called after the order of Aaron? (Hebrews 7:11 (King James Version)

    This chapter will talk in detail about how God uses anyone He wants, no matter what level of citizen others may have that person labeled as. All the previous chapters were accounts of how the process of life matures the Christian during his walk with Christ. These latter chapters will deal specifically with characters in the Bible and there encounters with the LORD. There is also a chapter dealing exclusively with the Lord Himself.

    I want everyone to understand that through a process each and every one of us will be perfected in Christ to help the body of Christ reach more souls and build up those that are in the body itself. I don't want to go to the Father with unfinished business like testifying about His love or helping to grow many in the body itself. Because I love the Lord, I also love my brethren enough to strengthen each and every one of them. The one thing that I have seen is the lack of understanding that there must be a process to reach those levels of glory that many people observe in those extraordinary saints. All glory comes with a price. Granted that each saint's price may differ from another, it still has to be paid. We all have to go through the refiners' fire to burn off all that useless, filthy, carnal-minded thinking that we possessed when we were without Christ. There are too many characters to discuss the many levels of progress that the saints have been through. Now, this is just counting those that are in the Bible itself. Many lived outside the written Holy Bible that could tell a story or two of their journey with Christ, which perfected them to the level

Mr. Charles Williams Jr

that they operated within. One thing is for sure; as long as we live, we will forever have another level to mature towards.

The Brains (Paul)

The Tyrant

And Saul was consenting unto his death. And at that time there was a great persecution against the church which was at Jerusalem; and they were all scattered abroad throughout the regions of Judaea and Samaria, except the apostles.[13] (Holy Bible KJV Acts 8:1) *And Saul, yet breathing out threatenings and slaughter against the disciples of the Lord, went unto the high priest, and desired of him letters to Damascus to the synagogues, that if he found any of this way, whether they were men or women, he might bring them bound unto Jerusalem.*[14](Holy Bible KJV Acts 9:1-2)

The beginnings of Saul upon the scene were not so pretty to the God-fearing people. Saul, in his mind, was right in his persecutions of the people of *that way* (Early Christians). Saul was not too different from the people of today actually. In Saul's understanding about God, it didn't make sense that this man Jesus was proclaiming his equality with God and any that follow that way. That being noted, Saul began his persecutions of the followers of Christ Jesus. Having much status within the region, he pushed that other areas would support his plight. I guess you can picture Saul in one way of a well-learned man that deserves recognition. Saul was a man that could well be a leader, even before his encounter with Jesus. He knew that he was of the stock of Benjamin, which meant he had papers of being a true Israelite. That is equivalent to someone today that may be related to the area's most well-known family, typically wealthy. That notoriety tends to make a person act like they are a little worthier than the next person. Saul was well cultured in many languages as well as scholarly equipped to know the Mosaic scrolls that ruled their society. Once again, this can be equivalent to an individual that behaves with more importance than the next person due to the certificates of achievements on their walls. All this could be counted worthy in man's sight, but dealing with Gods' wisdom it was not worth a *'hill of beans'* if not used to further the kingdom of God.

Now if you were on the other side of that 'table' and this young man Saul was throwing you into prison because of the gospel, then he was not so well liked. I have seen many individuals; both in Christ and without, that have persecuted people on account of the Gospel just for being later the ones that fight harder than the ones they initially persecuted. I often tell others when teaching the Word of God that many flaws arrive from our own ignorance. Please let me explain that ignorance shouldn't be an offensive word. I do realize that within this Western culture that it is often received within that manner. I, however, by no means ever commend that suggestion when teaching. I always explain that by saying one is ignorant is saying that one is unlearned within the specified area of conversation. I go on to explain for example that I scrutinized the Word and later on the LORD revealed truths to me to help me understand the Word clearer. This being said, we should understand that Saul did not have any revelations of Christ at the time of his persecutions. I wasn't totally awed by him at the first time of reading about him because I was just learning about God myself. My zeal for God was not closely measured to the zeal Saul had for right living, according to the Law of Moses, before knowing Christ. Later that zeal for right living, for the Law, was exchanged for the zeal for living 'for' Christ. Now I identify with that zeal for righteousness, and I speak with authority when it comes to righteousness.

As I mentioned earlier, I had come to realize that when I was on the untrained side of the table that I assumed that the Drill Sergeants were tyrants; when actuality they had a perception that I did not have at the time. This brings to my remembrance of Saul's zeal when dealing with issues with the LORD and not wanting Mark to travel on the upcoming journey with him due to his lack of understanding (faith) at that moment. Many people within Christ have strived with others due to lack of understanding (faith). I fell into that situation on occasion. Not so much with other people but within the WORD of God itself. I was very skeptical and didn't witness for a long time until I searched the scriptures enough that I could boldly confess Christ and know what I was standing on. You know that old adage 'If you don't stand for something that you will fall for anything'; I haven't been one to jump on 'bandwagons' too quickly.

Do remember that I am writing all of this to share with people that we have to go through trials and tribulations to understand a glimpse of God's wisdom. Whenever He decides to share His knowledge with us, we are blessed and should appreciate what little we do have. I have to say little because our (man) minds are finite compared to God's mindset which is infinite. The Bible says that His ways are not our ways.

If we really think about it, we all have come around people who at one time or another may have seemed coarse at first; but afterward, when time has set in, and that individual may then look to be better understood by you. That is how this man Saul came across, to me at least, when reading about his deeds before having an encounter with Christ for a better understanding.

The Transformation

'How can a brown cow eat green grass and produce white milk?'

And when we were all fallen to the earth, I heard a voice speaking unto me, and saying in the Hebrew tongue, Saul, Saul, why persecutest thou me? It is hard for thee to kick against the pricks.[15] The man Saul has now encountered the risen Son of God. Throughout the Holy Bible, there are many incidents whenever a man encounters a personal meeting with the LORD that there is a transformation that takes place; sometimes both in name and mindset. For example, Jacob which means 'trickster' was transformed into Israel: *for as a prince hast thou power with God and with men, and hast prevailed.*[16] Also, Abram was changed: *Neither shall thy name any more be called Abram, but thy name shall be Abraham; for a father of many nations have I made thee.*[17] As for Abraham's wife: *And God said unto Abraham, As for Sarai, thy wife, thou shalt not call her name Sarai, but Sarah shall her name be. And I will bless her, and give thee a son also of her: yea, I will bless her, and she shall be a mother of nations; kings of people shall be of her.*[18]

Leaving Saul for a second, I want us to understand that when we truly give our lives over to Christ, there should be a change in our lives. That old adage that says 'I'm not what I should be but thank God I'm not what I used to be'; should be a "ringing in the ear." If not you, someone should be able to notice the difference in your life. I must also add that if everyone loves you, then you might not be changed from within. The Light that should shine within you will be offensive sometimes to those who dwell in the Darkness. When a 'name' or mindset is changed in your life, you should begin transforming from that 'old man,' which was an enemy to God's ways, to a new creature that resembles the love that Christ Jesus performed while walking the Earth. He showed us how to walk in love.

So looking at that man once named Saul; who now is widely known as the Apostle Paul, born out of due season compared to the first twelve Apostles. This man that was once known as a terror to the 'Way,' first named followers of Christ, to now known as the man that has written over half the New Testament of the Bible. Paul was told that he had to labor much and he did.

Looking at the gift that God had instilled within him, we can now see the working of his gift even while his name was Saul. Let me go all the way back to the book of Jeremiah to show how God flows. In Jeremiah, the Lord says: *Before I formed thee in the belly I knew thee, and before thou camest forth out of the womb I sanctified thee, and I ordained thee a prophet unto the nations.*[19] We need to understand that God has a purpose for everything He does. Each and every person is born with a gift to edify the body of Christ. By the way, do you know your gift? Paul had the gift of zeal for righteousness; unfortunately, he misused it until his encounter with Christ got him on track.

Many of us are the same way. We use our gift for worldly gain and selfish motives. The book of James says: *yet ye have not because ye ask not. Ye ask, and receive not, because ye ask amiss, that ye may consume it upon your lusts.*[20]   I have always said that the worse tragedy in the world is to die without knowing your gift. Many of us may walk in our gift and never knew it because of where we walked. In other words, some people have become worldly rich from being a motivational speaker and never knew the LORD. They had the gift to speak in front of crowds, yet they would have been spiritually prosperous if they spoke in front of the body of Christ as a minister of the Word. Some people have become content with teaching the world how to count, speak, spell, etc. and yet never knew the Word of God. My, my, my how they could've brought many more people to the understanding of Christ if they followed Him. So many souls could've been won over by coming into the knowledge of the LORD. Or even looking at the woman in the neighborhood that was the sweetest person you will ever know. She always has the right word to say, or you will still see her smiling. What if she knew the LORD and worked as an usher in the house of God. Everyone who came to church would immediately be in good spirits upon entering into the sanctuary. This is why God gives gifts to the body to help it grow and sustain itself. That friend that is always there for an encouraging word; wouldn't it be sweet if they were saved and helped everyone they encountered and lifted up there soul to sustain their salvation. Just like Barnabas, whose name means son of encouragement, did for St. Mark after Paul's disagreement about working with Mark. Once again I have to say My, My, My!

    This is the transformation process that God deals with us about. Have you figured out about the brown cow, green grass, white milk concept? While you are thinking, think about how a black soul can be washed in red blood and become as white as snow? We have to remember God's thoughts are higher than our thoughts and God's ways are higher than our ways. If we keep this in mind and just use our gifts to edify the body of Christ, then we can be like what Jesus said for us to do; *seek ye first the kingdom of God, and his righteousness; and all these things shall be added unto you.*[21]

    We should by no means despise anyone for any reason anyway; especially now that you know that the very same person that is despised can be the very same person that God changes their lives to become a minister to the people. God can make way for that person to accomplish great things.

The Teacher

If you are an avid reader of the Holy Bible, you should be fully aware that one of its greatest teachers would be the Apostle Paul. Yes, the very same Saul that once persecuted the church. The same young man at whose feet they tossed their clothes upon stoning the disciple Steven to death for witnessing about Christ Jesus. The same Christ Jesus that Paul labors for so diligently. This is the after effect of the transformation mentioned earlier. This is the reason that I say we need to be more mature about handling conversations with people we may not agree with at the time because we do not yet know how God will change their lives later on.

Paul wrote over half of the New Testament, and I'm sure he affected several of the other writers as well. His spiritual son Timothy was equipped by Paul to minister the Word of God. Paul encountered Peter, another writer of the Word of God, which I know Peter was influenced by Paul's words. When you are a teacher, you will affect many people with your knowledge. Being a teacher of the world as well as spiritual, I know that what is spoken from me will be again voiced through those I've taught. Paul has expressed on all types of subjects from daily living as a Christian to why we should even be a Christian. He explains how to become closer to Jesus and also just who Jesus really is to us. One thing that Paul speaks on is how to suffer for Christ. This suffering is what brings about the maturity that the world takes notice of immediately. I say this because it is the most obvious lifestyle that is noticed among Christians. How we handle everyday life's trials is the forefront of our witnessing. It does not, however, strengthen our witness when we talk a changed lifestyle about love, and then we turn around and lose our temper towards a co-worker, boss, neighbor, etc.... while the worldly people look on. This is the 'biting of the tongue' mentioned earlier that should be done for Christ sakes and not ours. If only for our sakes, then we could be satisfied with cursing out someone and getting the last say. This action would not draw someone towards Christ but would drive them away: for this reason, Paul teachers on how to live for Christ through suffering, through denying ourselves for the greater of the people.

The Bronze (Samson)

The Baby

Behold now, thou art barren and bearest not, but thou shalt conceive, and bear a son...and no razor shall come on his head: for the child shall be a Nazarite unto God from the womb [22] *(Holy Bible KJV Judges 13:3-5)*

As mentioned earlier, God has put a gift in each one of us for the working of the body of Christ. This gift is given as early as being formed in the belly of your mother. Here from the book of the Judges, God is giving the children of Israel a deliverer as early as childbirth. Wow, it's just so amazing that God can provide us with our gift at the age of zero; yet we do not walk in our gift, if at all, until the age of forty for some. Israel can be identified as our nation, city, family, and friends of today. As I speak on this subject, I hope to convey a message to you that will get you down on your knees and pour out to God for Him to help you find your gift. Oh, what a tragedy if we never find that gift!

I told a young man just the other day that if he doesn't use the gift that is within him that he will never be truly satisfied. I mentioned that if he decides not to follow God and decides rather chase the world that he will not be satisfied and he will waste years if God gives him years, which he could be productive for the number one employer of all time. God empowers people to encourage, deliver, uplift, etc. others. We need to recognize this working and find out each and every gift he gives you.

I would like to reiterate my message to grow in the LORD. I am using a combination of my gift to teach, the gift of remembrance of the Word of God and experience of hard times in life as well as the blessings. I don't want anyone to lose out on true joy of living this life. If I can prevent any undue pressures of this world to make someone's life better, then I've done my duty by writing this book. I hope and pray as well that the readers of this book, as

I reveal scriptures, that the teachings will be taken up and blessings will fall onto lives as a result.

There is a specific scripture that is revealed in Judges that I want to bring forth. I definitely feel this topic would be a blessing if we heed to it. The topic is how we should start off raising our babies. In the thirteenth chapter of Judges, Samson's father, Manoah, says to the Angel of the Lord; *how shall we order the child and how shall we do unto him?*[23] *(KJV)* Another translation that I want to focus on reads...*what kind of rules should govern the boy's life and work?*[24] This is how we should address the Lord concerning our own children. If we think about it, who has been around the longest and should know very well how to raise children? The LORD has given everyone instructions on how to live accordingly, and he didn't leave out about how to rear the children. When we do according to what the LORD says we will allow room for blessings to come into our lives. I want your children to have blessings so you, the parent, will feel proud of your children.

    Samson grew in strength as the LORD began to take hold of him. Wouldn't we like to have our children being taken hold of by the ruling and supreme God Himself? Well, let this be the first step to making that wish come true. Start putting rules around your children to be governed by throughout the life in your home so when they become citizens, they will follow the laws of the land. We cannot escape this life without being governed by someone: rather boss, policeman, company rules, judge, road signs, store signs, etc.... somehow we will be governed.

    I want to leave this section with: *Children obey your parents for you belong to the Lord.*[25]

The Bully

Do you know someone in Christ that seems to brandish their gift frequently? It looks like every time you see them they are being boastful, past confident mind you, and you can even say prideful about their gift. This is the other extreme that I want to mention. Earlier I mentioned the tragedy of not knowing your gift; now I want to speak on the tragedy of abusing your gift. Jesus showed us early in His ministry how we should handle this situation. If you can remember when Jesus was lead into the wilderness and was tempted by the devil, Jesus dealt with the pride of life. Knowing that Jesus was the Son of God meant that even though they were on the highest point of the Temple; if Jesus jumped off, for the Scriptures says: *"He orders his angels to protect you. And they will hold you with their hands to keep you from striking your foot on a stone"*. He could have boasted. Instead, Jesus responded, 'the Scriptures also say, "Do not test the Lord your God."

Sampson knew his gift was his strength and flaunt it he did. Thank goodness God's ways are not our ways. God knew Samson would behave as he did and he still used Samson's gift to begin to break the bondage on the people of Israel from the Philistines. Samson used any excuse he could to torment the Philistines. He caused trouble to the Philistines all the days of his life. This is a touchy subject to teach, but I will try to tie Samson's life with ours today.

I by no means want us to use our gift uncontrollably with no restraints as Samson abused his. When we use our gift, we should bring the power of love from Jesus with us. Samson exposed no love with his gift of strength. Samson whipped on the Philistines as often as possible. If it wasn't their citizens, it could be their gates for example. Yes, Samson ripped the city's gate right along with the hinges and carried them away while leaving the city with no protection against an enemy.

Here are some examples of what I say about abuse of gifts: A prophet exposing many things dealing with an individual in front of many when some things were not meant to be revealed during that season. This prophecy could be devastating to that individual, especially when what is said is not the season of exaltation but a dire warning. A singer who wants the spotlight and begins to be uplifted in pride; a deacon that wants to get rid of the pastor and wants to pastor himself; a teacher that rules loudly about how to live life but refuses to live righteously himself; and a pastor that uses the pulpit to fuss and complain out of flesh to rule with an iron fist are examples. These things should not be so.

This is why I say that perfect is not pretty. For us to resemble Christ, we must suffer some truth about ourselves. We must be ready to suffer through stretching, through changing, some growing to make our light even brighter for Christ. The following chapter will break that bully of a man in Samson. So let's look at the walk of Samson in the flesh and compare it to the humble man of Samson that I will speak on in the following chapter.

The Bereaved

"But the Philistines took him, and put out his eyes, and brought him down to Gaza, and bound him with fetters of brass, and he did grind in the prison house."[26] *(Holy Bible KJV Judges 16:21)*

I know it may seem odd to name this topic 'The Bereaved,' but this is a normal feeling when someone dies, don't you agree? Well, keep in mind that this book is geared toward the spiritual mindset of people. Within the spiritual conversations of things, we die to the old nature of things to take on the new nature of Christ. The days of bullying the Philistines at his every whimsical was now over. Samson's days were now to be filled with humbleness.

This is the most forward subject that is to be explained as a Christian. Many people are not aware of the truth about growing in Christ. Too many people give their lives to Christ without knowing the cost at hand. Jesus mentioned in His Word to take up our cross and walk. In layman's term, we need to realize that giving up our old way will cause 'storms' in our lives. Letting go of habits, friends, family, etc.... has to take place in our lives to mature. Keeping old habits will not allow room for good habits to take over in our lives. If we want peace and change in our lives, we first must die to old ways of living. We must exchange the old man for the new man.

Samson's old ways had come to an end. Understand that even though his ways had succumbed to a halt, God's use of him had not. Samson spent a lifetime of trying to fulfill his gift by his own way of doing things, but he would soon see that God's way of using his gift would destroy more Philistines than Samson's whole lifetime of killing Philistines.

When we use the gifts that God has given us, when God wants us to use them, then we can be more productive according to God's

Perfect is not Pretty

plans. The sooner we move our selfish motives out of the way, the sooner the LORD can use us more effectively. If you read the book of Romans Paul tries to explain the old nature of man being dead while the new character of man should reign over the body. Understanding the death of the old man can be a bitter struggle due to the close attachment of our 'fleshly' desires. The sooner we understand that God's way would become more fulfilling; then we could end the struggle. Unfortunately, this is not how it works. Many people go on struggling for many years in the same situations when they could benefit more by laying that struggle down and just be bereaved about it for a short season. I say a short season because once they realize the better result of putting that struggle down. The profit from performing God's 'will' shall manifest itself before they know it.

Some struggles I put down many years ago. I don't even think on them now. Before studying the Word of God, I didn't understand how putting away some things would be more helpful to my own soul as well as others. Granted it was a sad moment, and many moments to be truthful when I had to resist doing what my nature had done for so many years. I was also saddened because I had to lose some companions along the way. I do understand that it can be hard letting some habits go, but when compared to the glory that God can give us then we should just have faith and let it go. We can possess many more blessings if we just let go and let God take over our lives. If we think about it, what mess have we created after all the years that we have been in control? Wouldn't it make sense to give God, our creator, a chance to run our lives? Even if we give Him a few months as a chance to change us, wouldn't it make sense to at least try Him? After all, what do we have to lose? If we couldn't get it right by now, I say try it and see. Be sad for a moment for putting that old nature to the side and pick up your cross and follow the Savior of your soul. The One who cared so much that He gave His only Son to save those who didn't know Him. That is love if I ever saw love before in my life.

Samson was bereaved for a season. He was bereaved long

enough to be humbled and to be able to see, for if not the first time spiritually. Although carnally blind, he could now see spiritually what God wanted for his life. After judging Israel for twenty years, God gave him his strength one last time; that in the death of Samson, he killed more Philistines in one hour than all that he killed during his lifetime.

The Beauty (Mary)

And the Angel came in unto her, and said, Hail, thou that art highly favored, the Lord is with thee: blessed art thou among women.[27]*(Holy Bible KJV St. Luke 1:28)*

The Beauty Within

Have you ever felt like you aren't special to this world? Have you felt like you are insignificant and how could you possibly make a difference? If you have felt like that, then join the millions of Christians that have journeyed to that very same crossroad. We really never know how important we are in this world until someone comes back around our path and mentions just how vital our interaction was to them. The point I want to raise is that if you know just who you have on the inside of you, then you should be joyful for that reason if nothing else.

Mary had a beauty inside her that would interact with this world and impact every corner of this world. Jesus mentioned that greater works would we perform through the Comforter He left with us. If we just learn to let the Lord have his way in our lives, we too would impact our society and cause eyebrows to lift and take notice. Jesus mentioned that His Word would not come back to Him void. If we would be molded by what He left inside of His followers, we could be powerful vessels for His kingdom. Mary was told at an early age that she would have the gift of the Holy God Himself within her. Mary had found favor with God just as we have if He has called you to become His son/daughter.

It is this favor that I want to begin speaking on. This very same favor will cause us to have something so beautiful inside that others can notice before you say a word that you are the child of the Most High God. People should come to you and say things like: "You have a glow about yourself, you are a Christian aren't you, you are a preacher aren't you, etc." Mary's beauty from within was so evident that when she visited her cousin Elizabeth that Elizabeth's baby leaped within her womb. When we are saved and set apart for God's use, there should be leaping in others' bellies about the gift that God has put within us. "*What is man that thou art mindful of him? Or the son of man, that thou visitest him?*[28] God has thought so much of us that He wants to dwell with us within this Holy Tabernacle that we call a body.

I want to encourage you that the God in you wants to express Himself to the world through you. God has given each and every person a special gift that if that person walks in that gift, the world will benefit from it. I am challenging each and every one of you to find that gift and run with it. If you are having trouble finding your gift, find a ministry, minister, or some type of godly fellowship to help you find that gift. The days are getting shorter, and we should redeem the time that is at hand and work while we can for the Lord; for Jesus said that *the night cometh when no man can work.*[29]

The Perfect Road to the Cross

As human beings, we can only see down the street a ways, but the one and true Holy God can see down the street and around the corner. I am sure thankful that I have Him in my corner. I'm hoping that all of you will get a little closer to Him through the writings of this book. I want to try and explain the walk Jesus had to take for us if we were ever to get back the fellowship that was once there with God in the Garden of Eden. This topic should not be taken lightly at all.

To understand the cross that Jesus had to bear, we must first understand the reason that He had to come at all. First, we must remember the fellowship that Adam had with God in the garden. Man walked with God and Oh how I know that had to be a beautiful thing! Could you imagine the beauty of it all? Can you see the immaculate habitat all around, the serenity, the energy from knowing without a shadow of a doubt that God loves you and He would be talking to you all of the time? I know I like the job that Adam had of managing the Garden with no sweating of the brow.

That fellowship was broken, and the enemy wanted to try and take as many souls to damnation with him as possible since his fate was already sealed. God had kicked Lucifer, the devil, out of heaven with no chance of repentance; yet when man sins, we can ask for repentance and still get back into fellowship with God. That being known, we should now understand that the enemy is not our friend. The enemy wants to take as many souls down with him as he can.   God is omnipotent, (all knowing), He immediately made way for Man to return unto Him. That way was through the cross or bearing that sin that Adam committed and nailing it to the cross. Because of that sin that Adam commit-

Perfect is not Pretty

ted, it was transferred through his loins to every man ever born. The enemy, the devil, knew that and had always tried to condemn man to the bondage of death which was the punishment of sin; *for the wages of sin is death*[30], but thank God the rest of that scripture reads: but *the gift of God is eternal life through Jesus Christ our Lord*[31].

God had already planned that Jesus was to be the sacrificial Lamb for mankind; although it may look as if Jesus was defeated by the carnal eyesight. So now you should know that the suffering that Jesus endured was because of the Love that God had for the world. This explains the passage in the Bible that says "*For God so loved the World that He gave His only begotten Son, that whosoever believes in Him should not perish, but have everlasting life.*[32] So the Cross was the final battleground to give man a chance to restore his fellowship with God. I say chance because it is a choice to follow God. It clearly states in the previous passage that one must believe in Christ to obtain everlasting life. It is nothing that God forces on Man, but it is a gift that He wants Man to receive. Have you received the gift?

A certain man encountered a homeless person and since he was a wealthy man he decided to bless the homeless person with a million dollar check to choose whatever he wanted or needed to do. That man could buy whatever he needs and probably anything he could possibly ever want because he had a million dollar check in his hand.[33]. That man remained destitute for the remainder of his life. You most likely would say why? The reason is simple; the man never cashed the check. This scenario is no different from someone having the gift available for everlasting life and never receiving it. God has done His part to save each in every soul. Our role is to receive the gift and live a life worthy of Christ. Please don't die destitute by directly not accepting the gift that Jesus brutally suffered on the Cross for you.

Jesus the Christ?

And there are also many other things which Jesus did, the which, if they should be written every one, I suppose that even the world itself could not contain the books that should be written.[34] *(Holy Bible KJV St. John 21:25)*

    With these last days of technology reaching all over the world, literacy has been prolific and at an all-time high. That being said we should really have no excuse to know the Lord a lot better than we do. Technology has exposed Jesus to the farthest of the once remote places of the world. Television has allowed even those that are still illiterate to know of Him. Jesus is the most famous man of all time throughout many centuries and cultures. His teachings have changed billions of lives.

Often I have started study sessions with a question about genealogy. I ask individuals to tell me their great-grandfathers' name. Some could not even tell me their grandfathers' name. Then I show, within the scriptures, how the Jewish culture could trace the genealogy of Christ back to Abraham and even back to Adam. That attention to detail should at least raise an eyebrow about this individual. Even other religions noted Jesus, although just as a great prophet and not of His divinity; so there still should be enough cause there that an eyebrow should be raised, wouldn't you think? At some point, we need to move out of the arena of self and broaden our horizons that there is possibly more truth in the Holy Bible than just what we know from growing up within our small town exposure of self. Without picking up the Bible or going to a local church, or even watching anything of the gospel on television, how much knowledge about self could you possibly rely upon? I started reading and asked myself what it could hurt to gather information?

    I just want to urge each and every one of you to investigate

this Man from God. It couldn't hurt the brokenness that we have already done unto ourselves. We might as well try Jesus; especially since so many others have claimed that He changed their lives for the better. We also can't overlook the way many have even fallen in love with such an individual that it supersedes any physical relationship that they encounter. I hope that thus far it has inspired you to take a peek at this world-renowned individual that just happens to be the Savior of the world. I am allowing Him to use me to help people every day to come closer to Him.
Using only the Holy Bible exposes six thousand years of Christ's Interaction with a man. On the surface of the scriptures, it may seem that Christ has only been around the past two thousand years, but more in-depth readings would show much longer. I am mentioning this to show you that it wasn't just one nation to bring this man about but thousands of years of speaking of Him before He manifested Himself onto the scene during the Romans' reign.

The book of St. John chapter one starting at verse one reads like this: *In the beginning was the Word, and the Word was with God, and the Word was God. The same was in the beginning with God. All things were made by him, and without him was not anything made that was made. In him was life, and the life was the light of men*[35]. It takes studying to understand some of the scriptures because much of it was written for those who diligently seek Him. I am exposing this right now to show you that God thought of you before you were even born and gave each one of you a gift to be used for His kingdom's sake.

We first must look at an obvious fact to understand this scripture. God the Father is a spirit. Also when we return to the book of Genesis chapter 1 verse 26, God said *let us make man in our image*; therefore man was first created in the image of God who is a spirit. God then fastened man with clay of the ground for a physical body and breathed the breath of life into the man that he would be different from all others creatures made. The mystery of St. John is unfolded in verse 14: *And the Word was made flesh, and dwelt among us, (and we beheld his glory, the glory as of the only begot-*

ten of the Father,) full of grace and truth.[36] As we, hopefully, see that Jesus was here the whole time as God Himself, but for our sake, He put on flesh and physically became the Jesus we know Him as.

The next question is why did He come in the flesh for us? This question can be answered once again by going back to the beginning, Genesis. We have all heard of the fall of Adam, but I genuinely don't believe people know what we indeed lost. Although on the surface, people seem not to see the impact of losing fellowship with God, the man at one time walked with God and was the glory of God. This fall that we take lightly separated us from the living God Himself. How much of a tragedy would that be, to actually live forever without the fellowship of the light of the World? God showed man physically through the practice of the sacrificing of animals to show that blood had to be lost for the remission of sin, to restore fellowship with God. Howbeit, animals, could only bring a temporary fellowship, while the blood of Jesus on the Cross was to bring eternal fellowship if we receive the gift. The more we read the Word of God it will be revealed more unto us that Jesus has been moving throughout history and the whole purpose of the Holy Bible was all about God/Jesus/Holy Spirit.

    I don't expect all to receive everything I just spoke on. My mission is for some to be enlightened so to pursue Jesus while it is yet day, because once again I must reiterate Jesus' saying that *I must work the works of him that sent me, while it is day: the night cometh, when no man can work*[37]. So choose today when you hear about Him to begin to follow Him. For those who are already following Him, be mindful of these last days and run this race as to win a prize.

LIST OF THANKS

KELLIE SARAI WILLIAMS

CHELSEA CENORA WILLIAMS

COACH GEE

COACH GATHEN

MINISTER DAN

LACRESHA HAYS

FORT JACKSON DRILL SERGEANTS

BISHOP ARNOLD OF SAINT MARK, LITTLE ROCK

MICHELLE HARVELL

LILLIE STANTON

---

[1]s The Merriam-Webster Dictionary

[2] The Merriam-Webster Dictionary

[3] The Merriam-Webster Dictionary

[4] The New Strong's Exhaustive Concordance of the Bible

[5] The New American Bible version of the Holy Bible

[6] The New Living Translation version of the Holy Bible

[7] *The Merriam Webster Dictionary – meaning number 2&3*

[8] *The Merriam Webster Dictionary – meaning number 1*

[9] *Holy Bible (Joshua 24:15)*

[10] I Corinthians 13:11 The Holy Bible (KJV)

[11] Isaiah 55:6 The Holy Bible (KJV)

[12] Mathew 16:26 The Holy Bible (KJV)

[13] *Holy Bible (Acts 8:1)*

[14] *Holy Bible (Acts 9:1-2)*

[15] *Holy Bible King James Version (Acts 9:5)*

[16] *Holy Bible King James version (Genesis 32:28)*

[17] *Holy Bible King James version (Genesis 17:5)*

[18] *Holy Bible King James version (Genesis 17:14-16)*

[19] *Holy Bible King James Version (Jeremiah 1:5)*

[20] *Holy Bible King James Version (James 4:2-3)*

[21] *Holy Bible King James Version(Matthew 6:33)*

[22] *Judges 13:3,5   King James Version of Holy Bible*

[23] *Holy Bible King James Version (Judges 13:12)*

[24] *Holy Bible New Living Translation (Judges 13:12)*

[25] *Holy Bible New Living Translation (Ephesians 6:1)*

[26] *Holy Bible KJV (Judges 16:21)*

[27] *Holy Bible King James Version (St. Luke 1:28)*

[28] *Holy Bible King James Version (Hebrews 2:6)*

[29] *Holy Bible King James Version (St. John 9:4)*

[30] *Holy Bible KJV (Romans 6:23)*

[31] *Holy Bible KJV (Romans 6:23)*

[32] *Holy Bible KJV (St. John 3:16)*

[33] *This is, of course, a fictional story used only as a scenario*

[34] *Holy Bible KJV (St. John 21:25)*

[35] *Holy Bible KJV St. John 1:1-4*

[36] *Holy Bible KJV St. John 1:14*

[37] John 9:4 The Holy Bible (KJV)

Made in the USA
Lexington, KY
13 March 2019